THE BEATLES FOR TWO

Arrangements by Mark Phillips

Cover photo: CBS Photo Archive via Getty Images

ISBN 978-1-5400-4815-8

HAL•LEONARD®

Visit Hal Leonard Online at
www.halleonard.com

Contact us:
Hal Leonard
7777 West Bluemound Road
Milwaukee, WI 53213
Email: info@halleonard.com

In Europe, contact:
Hal Leonard Europe Limited
42 Wigmore Street
Marylebone, London, W1U 2RN
Email: info@halleonardeurope.com

In Australia, contact:
Hal Leonard Australia Pty. Ltd.
4 Lentara Court
Cheltenham, Victoria, 3192 Australia
Email: info@halleonard.com.au

ALL MY LOVING

ALTO SAXES

Words and Music by JOHN LENNON
and PAUL McCARTNEY

20
24
28
32
36
40
D.S. al Coda
CODA

ALL YOU NEED IS LOVE

ALTO SAXES

Words and Music by JOHN LENNON
and PAUL McCARTNEY

Moderately (♩♪ = ♩♪ triplet)

18
21
24
27
30
33
1.
2.

AND I LOVE HER

ALTO SAXES

Words and Music by JOHN LENNON
and PAUL McCARTNEY

12
15
18
D.S. al Coda
(no repeat)
CODA
21
24

ELEANOR RIGBY

ALTO SAXES

Words and Music by JOHN LENNON
and PAUL McCARTNEY

13
16
19
23
To Coda
1.
27
2.
D.C. al Coda
(no repeat)
CODA

THE FOOL ON THE HILL

ALTO SAXES

Words and Music by JOHN LENNON
and PAUL McCARTNEY

Moderately slow, in 2

17
21
To Coda
25
29
D.S. al Coda
CODA

GOLDEN SLUMBERS

ALTO SAXES

Words and Music by JOHN LENNON
and PAUL McCARTNEY

16
20
23
26
29

HERE COMES THE SUN

ALTO SAXES

Words and Music by
GEORGE HARRISON

13
16
19
22
1.
25
2.

HERE, THERE AND EVERYWHERE

ALTO SAXES

Words and Music by JOHN LENNON
and PAUL McCARTNEY

16
19
22
1.
25
2.
28

HEY JUDE

ALTO SAXES

Words and Music by JOHN LENNON
and PAUL McCARTNEY

16
19
23
26
29
32
1.
2.

I SAW HER STANDING THERE

ALTO SAXES

Words and Music by JOHN LENNON
and PAUL McCARTNEY

18
22
26
D.S. al Coda
(no repeat)
CODA
30
34

I WANT TO HOLD YOUR HAND

ALTO SAXES

Words and Music by JOHN LENNON
and PAUL McCARTNEY

Moderately fast

16
1.
2.
20
24
27
D.S. al Coda
(no repeat)
CODA
30
3

I WILL

ALTO SAXES

Words and Music by JOHN LENNON
and PAUL McCARTNEY

18
22
26
30
34

LET IT BE

ALTO SAXES

Words and Music by JOHN LENNON
and PAUL McCARTNEY

20
24
1.
2.
28
32
37

THE LONG AND WINDING ROAD

ALTO SAXES

Words and Music by JOHN LENNON
and PAUL McCARTNEY

18
22
26
To Coda
30
D.S. al Coda
CODA

MICHELLE

ALTO SAXES

Words and Music by JOHN LENNON
and PAUL McCARTNEY

21
25
3
29
33
3
3
3
3
37
3
1.
2.

NORWEGIAN WOOD
(This Bird Has Flown)

ALTO SAXES

Words and Music by JOHN LENNON
and PAUL McCARTNEY

26
31
36
41
46
51

OB-LA-DI, OB-LA-DA

ALTO SAXES

Words and Music by JOHN LENNON
and PAUL McCARTNEY

Brightly, in 2

26
To Coda
31
1.
2.
36
42
47
D.C. al Coda
CODA
52

PENNY LANE

ALTO SAXES

Words and Music by JOHN LENNON
and PAUL McCARTNEY

Moderately

15
19
23
1.
2.
27
31

SHE LOVES YOU

ALTO SAXES

Words and Music by JOHN LENNON
and PAUL McCARTNEY

22
1.
2.
27
To Coda
31
D.S. al Coda
(take 2nd ending)
CODA
39
44

SOMETHING

ALTO SAXES

Words and Music by
GEORGE HARRISON

21
2.
24
28
1.
32
2.
D.S. al Coda
(no repeat)
CODA
36

WHEN I'M SIXTY-FOUR

ALTO SAXES

Words and Music by JOHN LENNON
and PAUL McCARTNEY

19
To Coda
23
27
31
35
D.S. al Coda
CODA
39

YELLOW SUBMARINE

ALTO SAXES

Words and Music by JOHN LENNON
and PAUL McCARTNEY

Moderately (♫ = ♩♪ triplet)

16
19
22
1.
25
2.
28
1.
2.

YESTERDAY

ALTO SAXES

Words and Music by JOHN LENNON
and PAUL McCARTNEY

16
19
23
26
29

HAL LEONARD PRESENTS

EASY INSTRUMENTAL DUETS

Start your duet playing experience with these fun songbooks! Over 20 easy duet arrangements for two instrumentalists are featured in each of these collections. Woodwind and brass editions can be played together as can the string editions. **Only $9.99 each!**

BROADWAY SONGS FOR TWO

22 showstoppers: Any Dream Will Do • Bring Him Home • Cabaret • Edelweiss • For Forever • Hello, Dolly! • I Believe • Memory • One • Popular • Seasons of Love • Seventy Six Trombones • Tomorrow • Where Is Love? • You've Got a Friend • and more.

00252493 FLUTE
00252494 CLARINET
00252495 ALTO SAX
00252496 TRUMPET
00252497 TROMBONE
00252500 VIOLIN
00252501 CELLO

CLASSICAL THEMES FOR TWO

24 favorite melodies from top classical composers: Air on the G String • Blue Danube Waltz • Canon in D • Eine Kleine Nachtmusik • Hallelujah Chorus • Jesu, Joy of Man's Desiring • Minuet in G Major • Ode to Joy • Pictures at an Exhibition • Sheep May Safely Graze • Trumpet Voluntary • William Tell Overture • and more.

00254439 FLUTE
00254440 CLARINET
00254441 ALTO SAX
00254442 TRUMPET
00254443 TROMBONE
00254444 VIOLIN
00254445 CELLO

CHRISTMAS HITS FOR TWO

22 terrific holiday duets: All I Want for Christmas Is You • Baby, It's Cold Outside • The Christmas Song (Chestnuts Roasting on an Open Fire) • Do You Want to Build a Snowman? • Feliz Navidad • Have Yourself a Merry Little Christmas • It's Beginning to Look like Christmas • Let It Snow! Let It Snow! Let It Snow! • Mary, Did You Know? • Rockin' Around the Christmas Tree • Silver Bells • White Christmas • and more.

00172461 FLUTE
00172462 CLARINET
00172463 ALTO SAX
00172464 TRUMPET
00172465 TROMBONE
00172466 VIOLIN
00172467 CELLO

HIT SONGS FOR TWO

22 mega hits: All About That Bass • All of Me • Brave • Can't Stop the Feeling • Grenade • Hey, Soul Sister • I Will Wait • Let Her Go • 100 Years • Royals • Shake It Off • Shape of You • Stay with Me • Viva La Vida • and more.

00252482 FLUTE
00252483 CLARINET
00252484 ALTO SAX
00252485 TRUMPET
00252486 TROMBONE
00252487 VIOLIN
00252488 CELLO

Prices, contents and availability subject to change without notice.
Sales restrictions to some countries apply.
All prices listed in U.S. funds.

ORDER TODAY FROM YOUR FAVORITE MUSIC RETAILER AT **HALLEONARD.COM**

HAL•LEONARD®

1217